This

WALKER BOOK

belongs to:

. . . .

. . . .

To Marla Morris Garrett – you are the light that inspires so many of us – **J.W.**

To Donna – discover the world with your own light – **A.S.**

Dr Jess Wade is an excitable scientist with an enthusiasm for equality. By day, she works in the incredible laboratories of Imperial College London, where she creates new materials to use in electronic devices. She spends her evenings trying to make science a more equal and fair place, celebrating the phenomenal contributions of researchers who are all too often overlooked.

Ana Sanfelippo studied graphic design at the University of Buenos Aires, specializing in typography. She uses acrylics and inks in her illustrations, and creates vibrant artwork for a variety of products, books and magazines. Ana lives and works in Madrid, Spain.

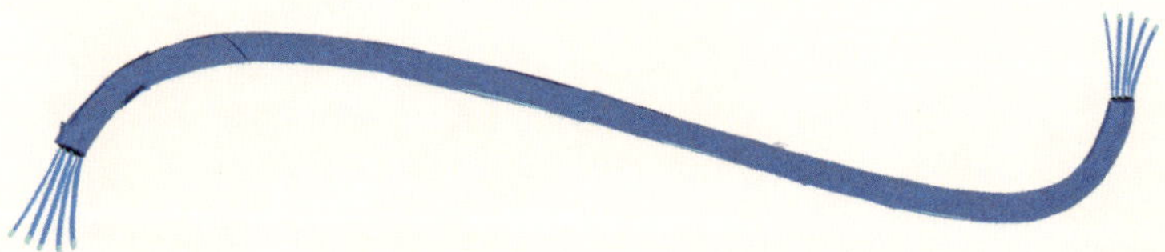

First published 2025 by Walker Books Ltd, 87 Vauxhall Walk, London SE11 5HJ • EU Authorized Representative: HackettFlynn Ltd, 36 Cloch Choirneal, Balrothery, Co. Dublin, K32 C942, Ireland. EU@walkerpublishinggroup.com • This book has been typeset in Alghera and Akaya Telivigala • Printed in China • British Library Cataloguing in Publication Data: a catalogue record for this book is available from the British Library • ISBN 978-1-5295-0602-0 • www.walker.co.uk • 10 9 8 7 6 5 4 3 2 1

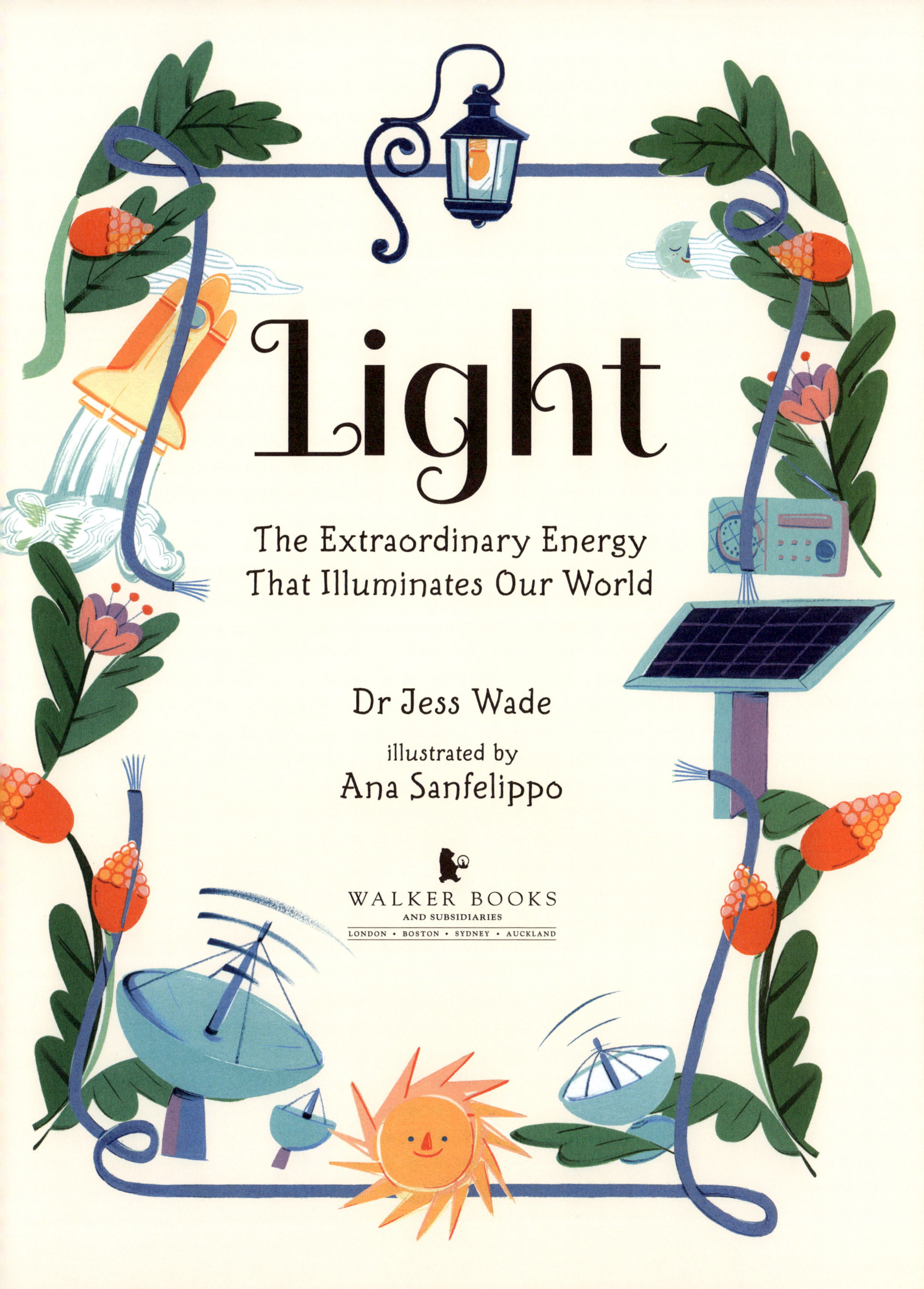

Light

The Extraordinary Energy That Illuminates Our World

Dr Jess Wade

illustrated by
Ana Sanfelippo

WALKER BOOKS
AND SUBSIDIARIES
LONDON • BOSTON • SYDNEY • AUCKLAND

Have you ever watched the sky at night?
Even when it looks very dark outside,
the night sky is never completely black ...
not even when the moon and stars
are hiding behind a thick blanket of cloud.

There is always **light** on our planet.

Most of this light comes from our nearest star: the sun. **Sunlight** makes life on Earth possible. Plants need it to grow, and all animals – including humans – need plants to survive.

And this isn't just about eating your vegetables! Plants put the precious gas "**oxygen**" into the air, which we need to breathe.

Of course, human beings need light from the sun for another very simple, but very important, reason: to see. For as long as we have existed on this planet, light has helped us to experience and make sense of our world.

The sun is our brightest and hottest light, but there are lots of others, too.

You can find all sorts of things that light up in nature:

NATURAL LIGHT:

Human beings have also come up with ways to bring light into our homes and neighbourhoods – and to help us get around after the sun has set:

But what IS light?

The answer might sound obvious, but it's actually a tricky question! Light is a kind of **energy** – one of many. (**Sound** and **heat** are others.)

There is light energy moving around our entire universe, and it travels in **waves** which can go mindbogglingly fast ... faster than our speediest sportscars, or trains, or planes. Even faster than rockets!

In fact, a light wave moves SO fast that, if you were going to try and keep up, you'd have to run seven and a half times around Planet Earth in a single second!

A wavelength is the distance between two identical points on two back-to-back waves.

As well as being incredibly fast, light waves travel in perfectly straight lines. And when they hit different kinds of objects, different things can happen.

Sometimes, the object blocks the light completely. This leaves a "**shadow**", which is a patch of darkness. A shadow's size and shape depend on how much of the light's path is blocked by the object.

You can test this for yourself by looking at your own shadow at different times of day.

At lunchtime, when the sun is overhead, your shadow is **shorter**.

But if you go for a walk at sunset, your shadow looks much **longer**.

But objects don't just block light.

Sometimes, the light waves bounce back – in one of two ways.

If the object is smooth and shiny, like a mirror, the waves bounce off at a similar angle, and in a similar pattern.

If the object isn't shiny and smooth (and most objects aren't!), the waves bounce off in all directions.

THE LIGHT IS "**SCATTERED**".

Sometimes, light passes *through* an object – like a windowpane. Light changes when it goes through an object: the light waves are slowed down, and end up sort of wriggling their way through. This means that they start to **bend**.

One of the best ways to see this in action is to use a kind of crystal, called a **prism**. Sunlight goes into the surface, wriggles on through, and all of a sudden you have:

A RAINBOW!

But HOW?

It's time to let you in on a little secret...

Sunlight might look white to human beings, but it actually contains a rainbow of colours: red, orange, yellow, green, blue, indigo and violet.

Every colour of light is a different wavelength: some are longer and some are shorter... From red (the longest) to violet (the shortest).

When sunlight goes inside a prism, some of the colours of light bend more than others – violet the most and red the least – so that they all spread out.

THIS IS CALLED "**DISPERSION**".

Things can look different colours to the human eye, depending on how they reflect and absorb light.

If something reflects all the different colours, and absorbs none, it looks white.

If something reflects red light and absorbs all the rest, it looks red.

If something absorbs all colours, and reflects none, it looks black.

These light waves are just the ones that human beings can see – there are lots of longer and shorter waves we *can't* see.

Over the years, scientists have discovered that these invisible waves can be useful! You may have heard of some of them already...

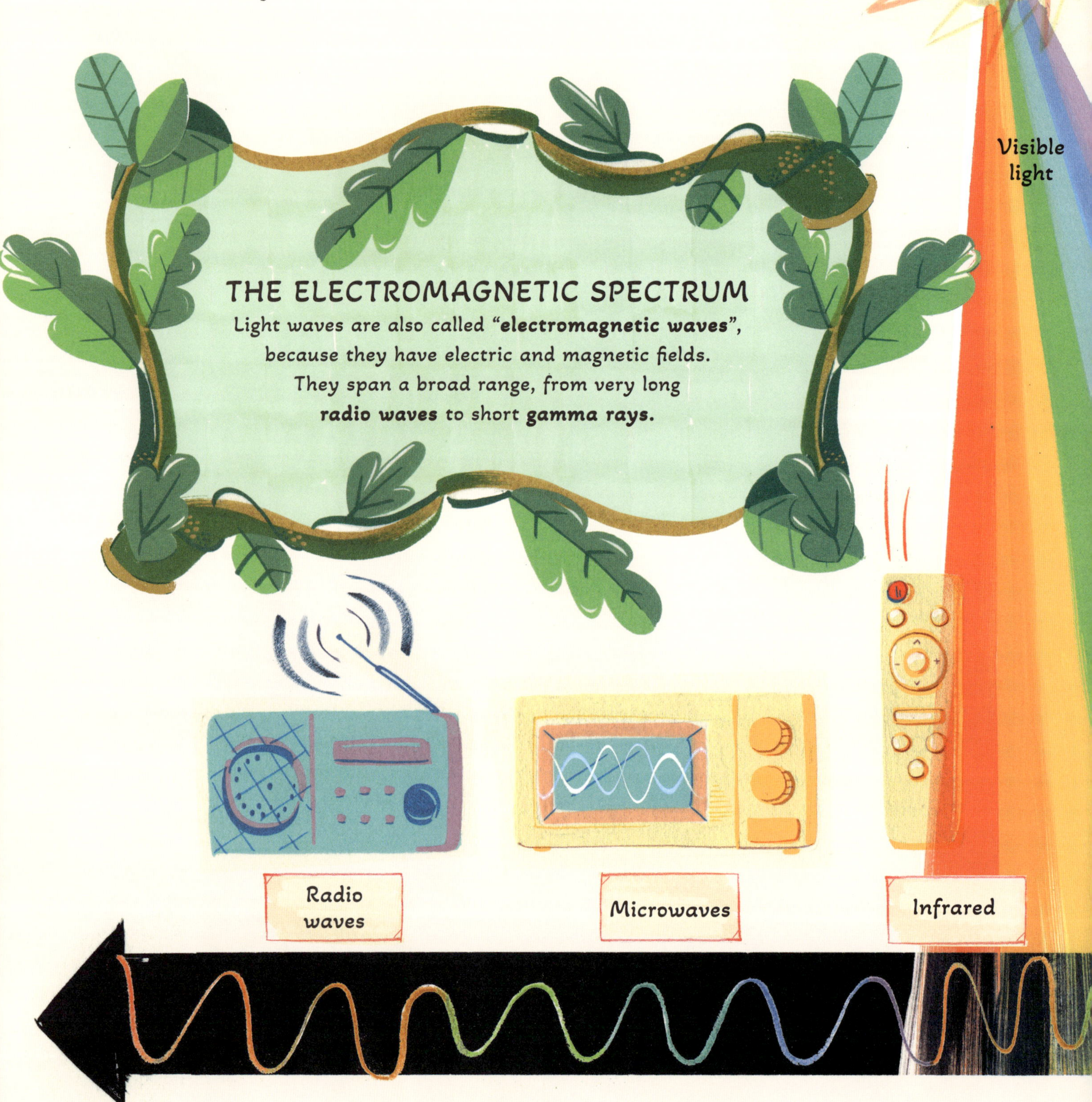

Some animals can see the waves that humans can't. Snakes can sense **infrared light** and bumblebees can see **ultraviolet** – in fact, this is how they find nectar to feed on. They look for ultraviolet patterns on flower petals – it's like a secret code!

Scientists from all over the world have been studying light for a long time – and have made some incredible discoveries. Now we're using light to connect people all around our planet and to help us understand and navigate our world.

The internet uses light! Our computers, tablets and mobile phones turn words and pictures into precise codes, which we can send down super skinny cables (as thin as hairs) as flashes of light.

Our computers waste lots of electricity and could be much quicker – scientists are working on "**quantum**" computers that send and receive information using special types of light. This would let us perform different types of calculations more speedily, and be better for the planet.

Aeroplanes and satellites can study how different colours of light shining on the Earth's surface bounce back. This is used to make detailed maps – of everything from our mountain ranges to the ocean floor.

We use **radio waves** to track aircraft, making sure they stay safe in the sky – and down on the ground, self-driving cars use different kinds of light to find their way around.

For years, doctors have used **X-rays** to take pictures inside our bodies, letting them see if any bones are broken. Now they also use high energy X-rays and **gamma rays** to treat diseases like cancer, targeting lumps (or "**tumours**") with light to prevent their spread.

We have also found ways to use the brilliant light we receive from the sun...

For generations, we have used the sun to grow crops and heat water. And now we use "**solar panels**" to turn solar energy into electricity (with "solar" just meaning "from the sun").

The sun is our biggest source of energy: every second, HUGE amounts of **solar** energy land on Earth. If we could capture it all, we would have 10,000 times more than we actually need.

We know that this energy is released by a particular kind of reaction (called a "**nuclear reaction**") which takes place in the sun... And so, scientists have been trying to create mini suns – right here on our planet!

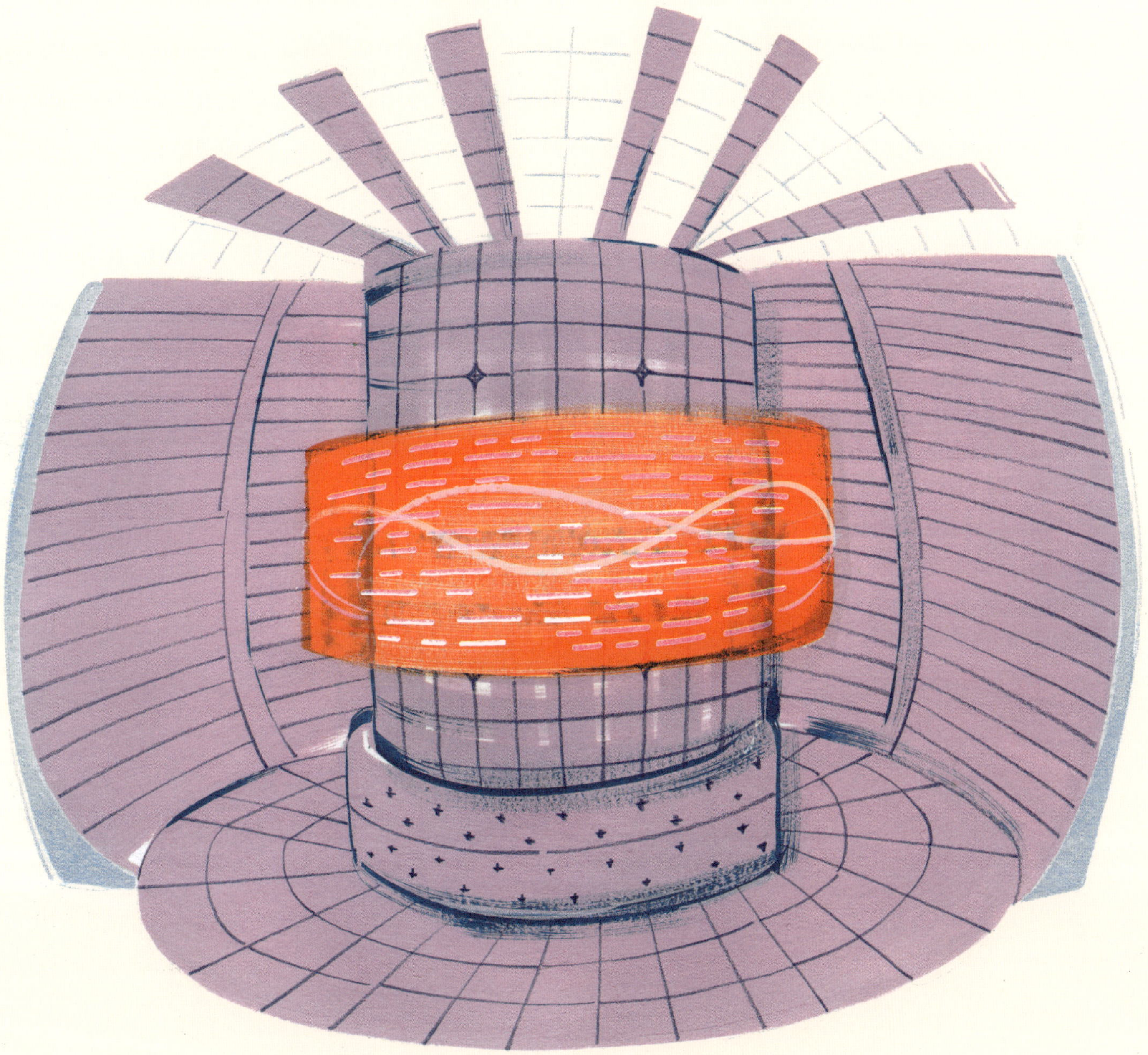

This is incredibly tricky to get right, but if we found out how to make these suns in a safe way, they would give us all the electricity we could ever want.

Light has changed how we live on Planet Earth in so many ways – and it has shown us a lot about our world. But it can also tell us a lot about our wider universe.

The universe is so gigantic that we are still picking up traces of the first light to ever exist: glimmers of explosions that happened billions and billions of years ago.

With a **super telescope**, we can also see that faraway stars shine in different colours... Each pattern of colours is like a fingerprint, showing scientists which gases are inside even the most distant stars.

We have a lot to learn much closer to home, too. There are some places on Planet Earth which have no light at all – like the deepest depths of the ocean.

If you took the tallest mountain on Earth and turned it upside down, the lowest part of the ocean still goes even deeper. And the sun's light doesn't reach very far under the water's surface: just ten metres down, there's only half of it to see by.

That makes it very hard to explore the mysterious worlds on the sea floor.

There's still so much left to find out! Even as you read this book, scientists are coming up with new ways to use light: to understand more about our world, and build a better one. And, who knows?

Maybe one day, YOU can help too...

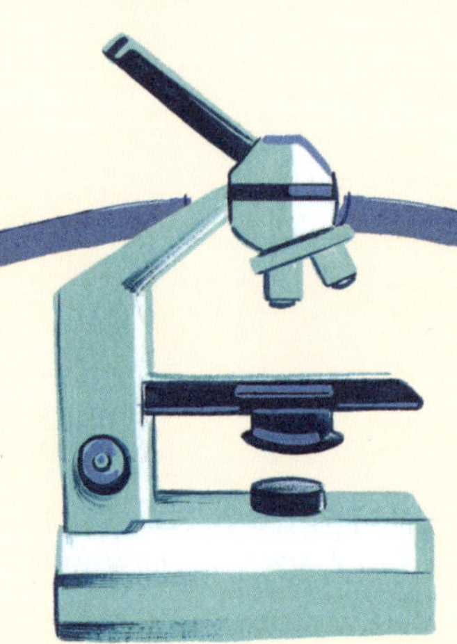

MORE ABOUT LIGHT

Sometimes light science is called optics and photonics. Optics is the branch of physics that studies the general properties and behaviour of light. Photonics involves using light to make technology, such as lasers, cameras, microscopes and solar panels.

Lots of different types of people work with light, from chemists to materials scientists, electronic engineers to physicists, and biologists to medical doctors. Some scientists create new ways to make and detect light, and some scientists use light to understand, explore and improve things.

MICROSCOPES AND TELESCOPES

Microscopes and **telescopes** use curved pieces of glass called lenses to manipulate light and magnify things that are small or far away. Microscopes are used to see tiny objects, like bacteria, cells and little creatures. Telescopes help us to see light that is far away, like distant galaxies.

LASERS

Lasers are devices that produce narrow beams of concentrated light. Inside a laser, atoms emit light that bounces backwards and forwards between two mirrors. The bright light excites other atoms to do the same, building up intensity that comes out as a laser beam. Lasers can be used to send internet and telephone signals along optical fibres.

SYNCHROTRONS

Synchrotrons are large machines that use a series of magnets to speed up charged particles, which produce intense beams of light. When the particles travel around the machine at high speeds, they emit powerful X-rays, which can be 10 billion times brighter than the sun. Scientists can use these X-rays to study atoms, molecules and even viruses.